The Golf Rules

~ Stroke Play ~

Learn the rules of golf by
watching others break them.

Richard E. Todd

Follow The Golf Rules at...

g Goodreads Author

www.TheGolfRules.com

The Golf Rules

– Stroke Play –

Learn the Rules of Golf by
Watching Others Break Them

The Story of Four Golfers,
Their Round, and the Rules of Golf

Introduction

The first set of golf rules were written nearly 300 years ago, in 1744. These rules were set to make the game equitable for all who play. Since that time, those few initial rules have grown and are now numerous and sometimes difficult to understand.

Golfers enjoy playing the game for many reasons. Some play for the camaraderie, the exercise, the competition, being outside, or for many other reasons. But regardless of why, every golfer is connected to the grand and ancient traditions and history of this game through the rules.

Few golfers know all the rules despite the desire to play by them. And the rules they do know are generally learned secondhand from others. Unfortunately, those that are explaining the rules were not taught correctly themselves. So the incorrect information is taken as truth and passed on to others. Not knowing the rules can limit your entitled benefits while playing and can create an unfair situation between you and your playing partners.

It is the intention of this book to bring the rules of golf to life, through stories, and make them easy to understand. While these examples may seem like fiction, know that they do happen, which is why the rule was written.

As you read through the book, the characters will encounter situations where a golf rule applies. This will be notated by the letter "C" followed by a number (example: C1.1). The explanation to that rule and situation can be found at the end of that chapter. Simply match the numbers and learn. At the end of the explanation, the corresponding USGA rule number, taken from *The Rules of Golf 2012–2015 Edition*, will be cited.

Decide for yourself if the characters made the right decision and refer to the rule explanation for confirmation and more information. Have fun learning the proper way to handle golf situations so you can enjoy every stroke in your round.

1

Chapter

Sunday morning, 8:00 a.m.

The quiet of the crisp morning is broken by the sounds of clubs rattling in golf bags as people walk in and out of the clubhouse and down the cart paths toward the first tee. The screeching of carts starting and stopping is mixed with the sound of drivers making contact with little white objects, curses being said immediately afterward along with gibing comments from others, and the bellow of the starter's voice over the public announcement system.

"Teeing off, Filler, followed by Burke."

Three golfers stood near each other by the first-hole tee box on the lush grass, still wet with dew, behind two other groups. Everyone was preparing for their round by filling pockets with wooden tees and divot-repair tools, storing scorecards and pencils, reviewing their golf clubs, stretching, swinging into the air, and sipping their morning coffee while waiting for their turn to tee off.

The booming voice was again heard, informing the crowds who had honors. "Teeing off, Todd group. Up next, Roeser, followed by Savina, then Voyk."

"Where's the kid?" asked Dick just as he turned around and caught sight of a fourth player running down the path, his golf bag swinging side to side and his clubs nearly falling out. "About time you made it. You're late. Did your mommy drop you off?"

Not even looking up, Nicholas grabbed his driver, a tee, and a ball. "I'm ready," he said. (C1.1)

"So match play? Ten dollars a hole?" Dick offered with a grin. (C1.2) "What do you say, kid? Does your allowance cover that kind of loss? No? Anyone else?"

After an awkward and silent moment, Dick spoke again. "Fine. We'll just play for bragging rights," he said as he pulled out a tee from a side pocket on his golf bag, causing the excessive amount of bag tags to rattle.

This was definitely not your normal group. The players really had little in common, outside of the love of golf and living in the same state. A few years ago, these golfers were matched up together on a busy holiday weekend. And as has happened with many other golfers, strangers became friends—or at least, golfing buddies.

The opening hole was challenging. It was a straight 419-yard par-4, with trees on both sides, a small valley running across the middle, and having a left-to-right slope to the fairway.

"I'll hit first," Dick spoke up, "since I have the lowest handicap." (C1.3, C1.4)

"Why don't I go first? I'm the youngest," Nicholas shot back.

But before the discussion could continue further, the sound of Dick's TaylorMade driver was heard. "That's how you do it. Down the middle, just the way I like it!" he smugly stated.

At that, everyone else just looked at one another; threw out their best rock, paper, scissors choice; and took their respective order.

Dick, or "Slick Dick" as the rest of the group liked to call him, was retired, played several times a week, was a club member at multiple courses, read all the golfing magazines, knew all the players, had the latest equipment, and was always willing to provide his opinion on everything. He was always showing up with new sticks—a new driver this week, a new putter next week, etc. Dick's clothes looked like a pro shop billboard. He had more logos showing on his clothing than most golfers could name. He had many bag tags from the well-known resort courses he visited and displayed them as if they were trophies.

Nicholas hit next. He placed his drive down the middle, thirty yards behind Dick's.

Nicholas was the youngest player, a tall and lanky teenager. Despite only playing for a couple of years, he had a fluid swing and a great love for the game. He didn't quite have the mental game down yet, and his game could fall apart after a few bad shots. Being young, he didn't have the power that will come as he grows, but what he lacked in distance he made up for in consistency. He played some nice, but older, clubs that he inherited from his uncle.

Richard was next to hit, and his drive went to the left side of the fairway, even with Nicholas's.

Richard is a high-handicap golfer. He doesn't play frequently enough to consistently score low but he has talent and a great respect for the game and its history. His equipment is similar, not new but they can produce distance and precise shots.

Last to hit was Howard. With his stocky frame lumbering over the ball, he teed off. His first drive of the day took a huge hook that went well into the dense trees on the left that bordered the edge of the course. "That's my breakfast ball, I'll take my mulligan," he stated as he quickly teed up and hit another ball, which managed to find the right side of the fairway. (C1.5)

Howard was in his early fifties. He played infrequently but had a new set of clubs every year and could really hit it long but not always straight. Golf was a diversion for him and his busy life. He and his wife had six daughters, all of whom played no sports. So golf was his testosterone time.

As the group walked down the fairway, Dick's voice was heard loudly. "So who agrees to bypass the rules today and we'll just have fun (C1.6)? No?"

"Richard, why don't you keep score (C1.7)?" Howard said as he continued toward his ball.

The group's second shots were uneventful, all landing around but short of the green, with Dick's being closest and on the front side.

Dick reached his ball first. (C1.8) "Tend the flag for me," Dick said to Richard who was walking across the green to his ball. As Richard held the flagstick, Dick lined up his chip and struck the ball, sending it fast at the hole. "LEAVE IT IN! LEAVE IT IN!" he yelled as Richard started to pull the flagstick from the cup (officially known as the 'hole'). His ball hit the flagstick and dropped within a foot of the cup. (C1.9) "Yeah baby! That's how you do it," exclaimed Dick as he walked over and putted his ball in the cup with his wedge. (C1.10) "Par for me."

Again, the rest of the group looked at one another, shook their heads, and took their respective turns to chip onto the green.

As Nicholas approached his lie, he pulled a second ball from his pocket and rolled it across the green. (C1.11) "Just getting a feel for the green. I didn't have time to practice putting before we teed off," he said as he took his stance and stroked his ball in the hole.

"Nice putt," Richard said, then lined up his own putt and dropped it in the cup.

Howard got his line and also one-putt to finish the hole.

"Pars all around. Looks like we halved that hole," said Dick. (C1.12) "Oh, wait, that's right, we aren't playing match play. (C1.13) Never mind, stroke play it is!" (C1.14)

Chapter 1—Rules Explanations

C1.1—Not only is it polite to be timely, but it's also the law—well, at least a rule of golf. You are required to be at the tee, ready to play, at your starting time; also known as a tee-time. If you show up within five minutes after your starting time, you are penalized two strokes for the first hole. If you show up more than five minutes after your starting time, you are disqualified from playing that round. R#6-3a

C1.2. Though technically not a rule, the USGA has no objections to gambling/wagering as long as all the players know each other, money is paid up front and is not an excessive amount, and the betting is optional. An 'amateur golfer' has special rules, with regard to gambling or wagering, to keep his status. R#A2—Policy on gambling.

C1.3—The order of play on the first hole is decided randomly, by lot. The person with the lowest score thereafter goes first (has "honors") on the next hole. R#10-2a

C1.4—Order of play does not include handicap strokes, only the actual number of strokes on a hole. R#6-2b

C1.5—Despite nearly every golfer knowing what a mulligan is and how to take one, there is no such rule. Every stroke counts. And in this situation, the ball hit into the woods counts as a stroke. Add a penalty stroke for losing a ball, and hit another ball from the same area (the teeing ground) for a total of three strokes. R#27-1a

C1.6—Sorry, players may not agree to exclude any rule or penalty. The penalty for agreeing to waive any rule is disqualification. R#1-3

C1.7—A person or persons should be designated as a marker, the person that marks down the scores, attests to the accuracy, and signs the scorecard at the end of the round. This person(s) doesn't have to be a player. R#6-6a

C1.8—After everyone has teed off, the player farthest from the hole hits next. If you can't decide who should play next, then draw straws. R#10-1b

C1.9—You may not strike the flagstick when someone is attending it, nor the person holding the flagstick. There is a two-stroke penalty for doing so. R#17-3

C1.10—You are allowed to putt with a club other than a putter. R#10-1c

C1.11—"Testing" the surface is not allowed when playing the hole. You can't test, or check, the conditions of the green by rolling a ball, or by roughing or scraping the surface of the putting green. There's a two-stroke penalty for testing. Although, after the hole is finished, you can test the green just played. R#16-1d

C1.12—*Halve* is a term that means "tied" in match play. This will be further discussed in an upcoming volume of *The Golf Rules* book. R#2-2

C1.13—One way to compete against others in golf is through match play. In this version, you win holes by having the least number of strokes on each hole. Match play score is stated that you are so many holes ahead or holes behind. If a player is more holes ahead than there are holes left to play, he wins and the match is over. R#2-1

C1.14—Another way to compete against others in golf is stroke play, in which whoever has the least number of strokes for all holes wins. R#3-1

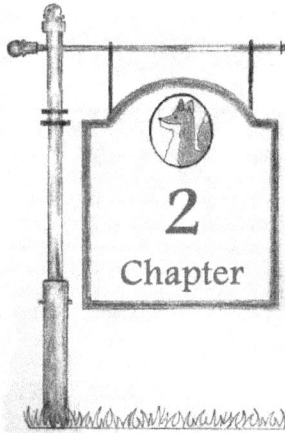

2

Chapter

The second hole was a short and straight par-3, wooded on both sides of the fairway. The back of the green sloped down into a pine tree wooded area.

Dick had honors and was standing in the tee box. Using his GPS to find the exact distance to the cup, he shared the reading. (C2.1) "It's 127 yards from tee to pin (officially known as 'flagstick'). Hmm, that's not gonna work for me. I hit this club 135 yards. Guess I'll just add a couple yards to my shot."

Dick then took several steps in the opposite direction from the green, placing himself just behind the tee box. He then teed up his ball and stroked a beautiful shot that landed a yard from the hole. (C2.2) "And that's how you do it," Dick stated.

Howard hit next. Playing his normal slice, he teed the ball to the far-left side of the tee box and stood just outside the teeing area. (C2.3) A quick stroke landed his ball just short of the green on the right side.

Richard's tee shot went long, flying over the green and down the hill into the woods.

Playing last and using his 8-iron, Nicholas landed his ball on the far-left edge of the green. "Pulled it," he said.

As he approached the green, Richard didn't immediately see his ball, so he began searching for it while Howard chipped onto the green, his ball stopping within a couple of yards from the cup.

After three minutes of searching the heavily pine-needled area, Richard's ball was found to be lodged under a fallen tree. Richard stated that his ball was unplayable and that he was going to pick up and drop his ball. (C2.4) He then grabbed his ball, stood straight with his arm out to the right at shoulder height, and dropped the ball, which landed softly on a cushion of dry pine needles. He then chipped it up to join the others on the green.

Nicholas putted first, leaving his lengthy putt a few feet short. He marked his ball and stepped back.

"I think your putt is gonna break about here," said Dick to Richard as he pointed to a spot on the green while Richard was lining up his putt. (C2.5)

Richard rotated his body clockwise a few degrees and rolled the ball into the center of the cup. "Thanks," he said.

Nicholas replaced his ball, picked up his marker, and sank his putt for par.

Howard then dropped his putt for par.

Dick tapped in his putt for birdie. "I'm hunting birds today," he said as he walked off the green toward the next hole.

Chapter 2—Rules Explanations

C2.1—You must not use any artificial equipment to help gauge distances. The penalty for breaking this rule is disqualification, unless a local rule allows devices for measuring distances. R#14-3b

C2.2—You must play the ball from within the teeing ground, defined as a rectangle two clubs deep in which the tee markers define the front side and its length. The penalty for hitting outside the teeing ground is two strokes, and you must correct any error of hitting outside the teeing ground before completing the hole. If you don't correct the error by going back to the teeing ground and re-hitting your shot, then you are disqualified. R#11-1(1)

C2.3—You can stand outside the tee box, but the ball has to be in the teeing ground when the stroke is made. R#11-1(2)

C2.4—As long as your ball isn't in a water hazard, you can claim the ball as unplayable. By doing so, you are saying, "There's no way I can hit this ball out of its lie." If you take the option, you can—for one penalty stroke—pick up the ball and either drop it within two club lengths of where your ball lies or on a line to the hole beyond where your ball lies or re-hit from where the ball was last played. Remember, you can never drop closer to the hole than from where you were. R#28c

C2.5 — You can't give advice or ask for advice from anyone other than your partner or your caddie. If you ask for advice, you are penalized two strokes. If you give advice, even if it's unsolicited, you are penalized two strokes. If you are given advice but did not ask for it, you, as the receiver, are not penalized but the person that gave the advice is penalized; even if you use the advice. So keep your suggestions to yourself. R#8-1a,b

~ Richard E. Todd ~

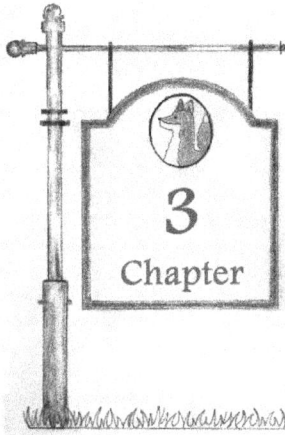

3

Chapter

"This hole plays short for a par-4. Since there's no room for error with these trees lining the fairway, I'm playing it safe and leaving the driver in the bag. Better to be short off the tee than in the woods on either side," said Dick as he stared into his golf bag and ran his hands over his clubs.

"Are you going to choose soon? How many clubs do you have?" asked Howard.

"Seventeen. I picked up a few new wedges and haven't decided if I'm keeping the old ones or the new ones. I plan on playing them all today to decide. (C3.1)

Grabbing a 3-wood, Dick let one fly down the left side of the fairway, settling on the short grass near the trees.

Howard, playing a fairway wood, put his drive just behind Dick's.

Richard did the same with a long iron while Nicholas landed his drive just at the tree line.

As they headed up the fairway, it was found that Howard's drive had landed in an unrepaired divot.

"This is unacceptable. They need to keep the grounds in better shape (C3.2)," Howard said as he took his club and rolled the ball out of the divot. (C3.3) Taking his hybrid, he made a smooth swing and solid contact, sending his ball flying onto the front of the green.

Richard was next up. Having no problem with his lie, he hit a clean 5-iron and settled his ball on the left side of the green.

Nicholas also had no problem with his lie, but coming up too early on his swing, he topped the ball, sending a worm-burner just fifty yards down the fairway. Angrily, Nicholas walked up to his ball and pitched it onto the green, close to the hole.

Taking a stance for his second shot, Dick found that the branches from a nearby tree were hitting his head. Reaching up with both hands, he broke off the branch that was brushing him and blocking his view of the hole. (C3.4) Taking a long and slow swing, he landed the ball nicely on the green.

Once on the green, Dick and Howard headed to their lies. Reaching in their pockets, they each pulled out ball markers and placed them behind their golf balls. (C3.5)

Richard, being in a hurry, bent down, grabbed his ball, rubbed it on his pants to remove any dirt or grass, and replaced it in one quick and smooth motion. (C3.6)

Without much excitement, each player took his turn and putt out for par.

Chapter 3—Rules Explanations

<u>C3.1</u>—You can't have more than fourteen clubs in your bag. If you do have more than fourteen clubs, then a penalty of two strokes for each hole played is applied, with a maximum of four total penalty strokes. R#4-4a

<u>C3.2</u>—As a general rule, you must play the ball as it lies—even if that means the ball is not in a perfect position. R#13-1

<u>C3.3</u>—You can't "improve" your lie, your swing area, your stance, the line of play, or any area you intend to drop a ball. Doing so will cost you a two-stroke penalty. R#18-2a

<u>C3.4</u>—This falls under "improving your lie." You can't move, bend, or break anything growing or fixed when playing the ball. Add a two-stroke penalty for breaking this rule. R#13-2

<u>C3.5</u>—On the putting green, you are allowed to mark and lift your ball and even clean it. R#16-1b

<u>C3.6</u>—Remember, you must mark the ball before you lift it. Failing to mark your ball before you lift it adds a one-stroke penalty. R#20-1

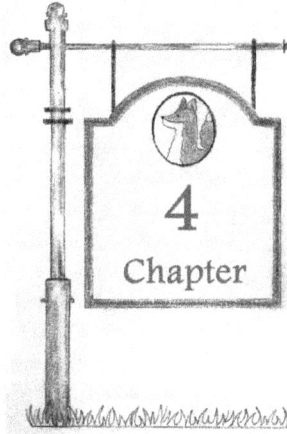

4
Chapter

The fourth hole was a par-4, playing to an elevated green. It played straight, with trees lining both sides of the fairway.

Being a lefty and having a strong fade, Dick moved to the far-left side of the tee box. A branch hung low over the teeing area just above his head. "They should have trimmed this back," Dick said as he pulled up the tee box marker and placed it a yard forward. (C4.1) He then reteed his ball and let a beautiful fade land in the middle of the fairway. "Beautiful," he said, as he replaced the marker to its original spot.

Addressing the ball next, Nicholas started his waggle. During this preshot routine, he bumped the club into his ball and knocked it off the tee. (C4.2) He looked back at the group sheepishly.

"That's one stroke," Dick said with a smirk.

Nicholas reteed the ball and took his swing, making contact and sending the ball to the center of the fairway, just short of the two-hundred-yard marker.

Howard hit next. Taking his driver back farther than normal for that extra power, he swung the club but only grazed the ball, knocking it to the ground. (C4.3)

"That's one stroke for you too," Dick chortled.

"Whatever," said Howard as he picked up the ball, reteed it, and took another stroke that made solid contact with the ball and landed his drive in the left side of the fairway. (C4.4)

Richard took his turn and drove down the right side of the fairway, heading for the brush-lined out-of-bounds stakes.

"Oh, that's not looking good," Dick said as everyone watched the ball land in the rough and take a big bounce right into the brush. It resembled a rabbit darting into his hole.

"I agree. I'm going to play a provisional," Richard said as he teed up another ball. (C4.5) "Maybe I'll get lucky and find my first shot."

Another stroke and the ball went sailing in the same general direction but managed to stay in the fairway.

Heading down the fairway, Dick and Howard found their balls side by side. Due to the height of the grass and the way the balls landed, it wasn't clear whose ball belonged to whom.

"I must be the one farther because I hit my shot real solid," said Dick confidently.

"Yeah, I don't think so," stated Howard as he reached down, stuck a tee into the ground near to and lifted the farther ball, and inspected it for his trademark radioactive symbol made with a red Sharpie.

"Yup, it's mine," Howard stated as he placed it back where it had been. (C4.6) He tried taking his stance, but his right foot was in a small rut in the ground. Dragging his foot back and forth, he filled in the area and, playing his hybrid, hit his ball just short and right of the green. (C4.7)

"This must be me then," Dick said as he checked out his lie. His ball was sitting nicely on the grass, but a small clump of dirt was directly behind his ball. With a quick stomp of his foot, he smashed the dirt flat. (C4.8) Noticing another small clump of dirt a foot to the side of his ball, he also tamped that ground flat. (C4.9) Dick then took his stance and stroked a beautiful 3-wood, landing the ball on the edge of the green.

Richard went to the edge of the woods where his ball was last seen. With help from Nicholas, he searched the area for five minutes, looking for his errant tee shot. (C4.10) Not finding it, he abandoned the search and went to play his provisional ball. Choosing a 5-iron, he landed his shot just off the green, coming to rest on the hillside lie.

Nicholas played next, landing his second shot on the green.

For his third shot, Howard, having a short chip, put his ball on the green too.

Approaching his lie, Richard found his ball resting against a sprinkler cover. Being allowed relief from the obstruction, he dropped within one club length. Due to the steep angle of the elevated green, the ball continued down the hill after it was dropped, coming to rest nearly twenty feet away.

"That's quite a roll," Howard said. "Try that again." (C4.11)

Richard re-dropped his ball, but it rolled away again. He then placed the ball by setting it near the sprinkler but giving himself room to swing. (C4.12) Richard then chipped to a few feet from the flagstick. Howard went to his ball, ready to putt, but found his ball resting on a drainage-hole cover. (C4.13) Howard bent down, lifted the ball, and set it an inch to the side of the cover. He then started looking around to see whose turn it was when he noticed Nicholas wasn't on the green.

"Hey, what are you guys doing over there?" Nicholas yelled from a nearby green. "Isn't this our hole?" he asked.

"You're on the wrong green," Howard said. (C4.14)

"Pick up your ball and drop it off the green and hit it here," Richard stated.

Doing as directed, Nicholas picked up his ball, walked to the edge of the green, and dropped the ball. Upon hitting the fringe, the ball bounced and rolled back onto the green. (C4.15)

"What do I do now?" Nicholas asked.

"Drop it again," Richard replied.

Nicholas re-dropped the ball, this time with success. He then pitched it to the proper green.

Howard then putt out for par while Richard sank his putt for bogey. Nicholas one-putt for par, and Dick drained his putt for birdie.

"And that's how you do it," Dick said as he walked off the green.

Chapter 4—Rules Explanations

C4.1—Tee markers are to be treated as fixed for the first stroke on a hole. Moving them is against the rules, and doing so adds a two-stroke penalty. R#11-2

C4.2—If a swing was not intended at a teed ball, such as a practice swing, and the ball is knocked off, you are allowed to re-tee it without penalty. R#11-3

C4.3—Even though the stroke only grazed the ball, the intent was to hit it farther. Once contact was made, that ball was in play and the stroke counted, and he was required to play from where it landed—even though it had traveled only a couple of inches. R#18-2a(i)

C4.4—Picking up the ball, when not permitted, incurred a one-stroke penalty for touching the ball. The ball was also moved back to the tee, which constituted choosing a different option, that of stroke and distance. This made his first stroke count. Add a penalty of one stroke, and the new tee shot is his third stroke.

C4.5—A provisional ball is hit when you aren't sure if the ball just played can be found or the ball may be out of bounds. This option isn't available if you believe your ball to be in a water hazard. If the first ball is found within five minutes, you play that one. If it isn't found within the time frame, you play your second ball, the provisional, and count the first stroke and add one penalty stroke. R#27-2a

C4.6—A ball may be lifted for verification, after it's marked, when not on the putting green. Before doing so, you are to inform your opponent or marker. The ball can't be cleaned and must be placed exactly where it was found. R#12-2

C4.7—You are allowed to stand firmly but not allowed to alter the conditions of the playing ground. This is known as building a stance. Changing the playing conditions incurs a two-stroke penalty. R#13-3

C4.8—You are not allowed to improve the area of your intended stance or swing. In this example, Dick flattened the clump of dirt to help his swing. Doing so penalized him two strokes. R#13-2

C4.9—You are not allowed to do anything with the intent to change the outcome of the ball flight or your swing path.

In this case, changing the condition of the course by smashing down the clump of dirt did not alter the swing path nor the flight of the ball but was only done to care for the course. No penalty here. R#1-2

C4.10—You are allowed five minutes to search for your lost ball. If it is not found or identified within five minutes, you must play a new ball from where the original ball was last played or any provisional ball played. Count the original stroke and add a one-stroke penalty before hitting again. R#27-1c

C4.11—If you drop a ball and it rolls more than two club lengths, then you must re-drop the ball. There is no penalty for having to re-drop the ball. R#20-2c(vi)

C4.12—If you re-drop a ball and it rolls outside the area that it must come to rest in then the ball must be placed as near as possible to the spot where it first struck the course when dropped. R#20-2c

C4.13—You are allowed relief from immovable obstructions when on the putting green. Simply pick up the ball and place it at the nearest point of relief with no penalty. Note that the nearest point may be off the green. R#24-2b(iii)

C4.14—If you end up on the wrong putting green, you must take relief without penalty. You are not allowed to hit off a wrong putting green. R#25-3b

C4.15—If you drop a ball and it rolls onto the putting green, you must re-drop the ball. There is no penalty for having to re-drop the ball. R#20-2c(iii)

~ Richard E. Todd ~

5
Chapter

The elevated tee box on the fifth hole had a breathtaking view. The fairway meandered down a hill, which was sparsely wooded on both sides, into an open area that faced a large green with sand traps (officially called bunkers) on each side and was open to the back. A small brook ran in front of the green to protect it from aggressive shots.

Dick had honors. He teed up his ball and hit it down the middle of the fairway, where it came to rest near the 150-yard marker.

Howard hit next and had the same result, landing near Dick's ball.

Richard's drive found the right side of the fairway while Nicholas's drive found the left.

Howard approached his ball for his second shot as Dick stood nearby and watched. Playing a smooth 8-iron, Howard hit it just over the brook, short of the green.

Dick looked down and asked Howard what ball he was playing.

"A Pro-Z with three red dots. Why?" asked Howard. (C5.1)

"Because that's what I'm looking at here! You hit my ball, you numbskull. (C5.2) Now run up there and get it," Dick said.

After a quick jog, Howard returned. "Here," he said through panting breaths as he dropped the ball (C5.3) near the original spot (C5.4).

Dick then took his address and pitched the ball to the green.

Howard, playing his correct ball, pitched it up to the green as well.

Richard and Nicholas, each playing from opposite sides of the fairway, took their turns. Both landing their golf balls in the right-side bunker.

Nicholas and Richard converged and walked to the trap. Neither ball could be identified as they were partially embedded and covered with sand. Richard stuck a tee next to the closest ball to mark the location then gently brushed some sand off it, just enough to see the manufacturer and his identifying mark, being careful not to move the ball. (C5.5).

"This is mine," he called as he sprinkled a little sand back on it. Addressing the ball, he then took a practice swing at the ground (C5.6), covering himself with sand. After brushing himself off, he addressed the ball and again took his swing. The club gracefully lifted the ball and dropped it six feet from the cup. Turning around, Richard grabbed the rake and proceeded to smooth out the sand, erasing all evidence he was there. (C5.7)

Nicholas entered the bunker. Taking his stance, he began to twist his feet back and forth to dig in. (C5.8) He then proceeded to blast his sand wedge, landing his ball five feet from the hole.

Howard's first putt was short, but he was able to sink it with his second putt.

Dick went a foot long on his attempt, then putt in for par.

Nicholas and Richard both one-putt for par.

"Did you have a four or a five on that hole?" Howard asked Nicholas.

"Five," said Dick (C5.9), "I always keep track of my opponent's strokes."

"It was a four. Nice par, Nicholas," stated Richard. "Don't listen to him."

"Good hole, all," said Howard as they headed to the next tee.

Chapter 5—Rules Explanations

C5.1—You should put an identifying mark on your ball. It's your responsibility for playing the correct ball. R#6-5

C5.2—You can't hit someone else's ball. Doing so incurs a two-stroke penalty. Furthermore, you must correct your error on that hole before completing it or be disqualified. R#15-3b

C5.3—The ball can only be placed by its owner, the person playing the ball, or the person who moved it. If you let someone other than those allowed to place your ball, then add a two-stroke penalty to your score. R#20-3a

C5.4— If the exact spot can't be determined, it must be dropped. If the spot was marked or can exactly be identified, it must be placed. If the ball is dropped when it should have been placed or placed when it should have been dropped, the penalty is two strokes. R#20-3c

Furthermore, If the ball that was supposed to be dropped is dropped by the wrong person or in the wrong manner (over the shoulder or tossed, for example) the penalty is one stroke.

C5.5—Normally, touching the ball, especially in a bunker, is not allowed. In identifying the ball, though, it can be done as long as it's marked, not moved, and the lie is recreated. R#12-1a

C5.6—When in a hazard, you can take a practice swing as long as your club doesn't touch the sand—not even just a little. Touching the sand is considered "testing the conditions," and doing so incurs a two-stroke penalty. R#13-4b

<u>C5.7</u>—After you have played your shot and hit the ball out of the bunker, you can smooth the sand without restriction. R#13-4-ex2

<u>C5.8</u>—You are allowed to dig into the sand to firmly take a stance. R#13-3

<u>C5.9</u>—There is no penalty in stroke play for providing incorrect information on your score until the entire round score is turned in. R#9-1

With that said, it's only proper etiquette to give accurate information if it's known.

6

Chapter

A waste area, composed of uneven ground and rocks and tall weeds, was directly in front of the sixth hole white tee box. It stretched to the forward tee box and was the full width of the fairway.

"Watch this," said Dick as he teed up a ball and smashed his drive at least fifty yards farther than normal. "I was saving that trick for the proper time," he said as he removed a piece of metal he taped to the face of his club (C6.1).

Howard, playing for his slice again, teed up on the far-right side of the tee box. Feeling this wasn't enough to offset his ball flight, he teed his ball farther right, just outside the tee box marker, but kept his stance in the defined tee box area (C6.2). A smooth swing landed his ball just inside the out-of-bounds markers.

Up next was Nicholas, who topped his drive, sending it straight into the waste area.

"You're shot didn't even reach the lil' kids forward tees," yelled Dick. "Maybe you should get a set of junior clubs."

Nicholas didn't even acknowledge the jab but smoothly pulled a ball from his pocket, reteed, and smacked a nice drive down the middle (C6.3).

Richard, playing last, teed up his ball and, with as much power as he had, swung. The ball took off fast but wobbled back and forth as it erratically flew, landing in the middle of the fairway but well short of his normal shot.

"That can't be good," said Howard as he and the others headed toward their respective lies.

After reaching his lie and having had seen the erratic flight, Richard felt something was wrong with his ball and picked it up to inspect it (C6.4). Seeing a nice big smiley face cut on the cover, he reached in his golf bag and replaced it with another ball, setting it on the original spot (C6.5). Then, using his 7-iron for his second shot, he landed his ball in the middle of the brook that was protecting the green.

Howard found his ball next, covered with mud and grass. "I can't hit this ball, it's unfit for play," he said as he picked up the ball and substituted it, in the same spot, with a new ball. (C6.6). Grabbing a 5-iron, he sent the ball on a nice flight that ended in a big splash as the ball landed in the same brook where Richard had just landed his ball.

Nicholas found his ball. Unfortunately, it was covered with twigs. "Can I get a free drop?" Nicholas yelled out (C6.7).

"Do I look like a rules official? You need to know the rules, kid," Dick said.

Nicholas looked back down at his ball. The lie resembled a solitary version of tiddlywinks. He started moving the twigs one at a time, ever so cautiously as he cleared the debris (C6.8). Choosing his 5-iron, he hit his ball over the brook, short of the green.

Dick took his turn and, playing a nice fade, landed on the green.

"I'm dry," stated Dick as he reached the putting green.

"I'm near the fringe," said Nicholas.

One ball was clearly visible under the water. Richard picked it up for verification. Seeing his familiar green stripe marking (C6.9), he declared, "It's mine."

Howard, noticing an area of the brook with a cloud of disturbed silt, started fishing around the bottom with his wedge (C6.10). After a moment he felt something. He stuck his hand in the water, pulled out a ball, and identified it as his. "Yup, here I am."

Richard, whose ball was only in an inch of water, chose to play it as it lay. After setting the ball back in the water, he took his wedge and, taking an awkward stance with one foot on the dry bank and the other on a rock in the creek, started his backswing. Just as the club reached the top of its arc, he noticed that the current moved his ball a fraction of an inch. Still in a good lie, he finished his swing, sliding his club into the water and under the ball, sending it out of its watery position and landing it on the green (C6.11).

Howard, having a lie in deeper water, chose to take the penalty and a drop to a dry area (C6.12). Backing up a few yards away from the rocky area near the creek, he dropped his ball and played from there. A nice wedge put him on the green, eight feet away from the cup.

Nicholas, not liking to putt from off the green long distances, chose his lob wedge to play the shot. His swing sent the ball on a high arc, landing it ten feet from the cup.

Dick walked up to his ball, which was near the hole. "Time to use my special ball marker," he said as he put down a metal disc the size of a jelly-jar top directly behind the ball. "I won this in a scramble for low score (C6.13)."

"You sure it was a prize? It looks like a Frisbee," Howard said as he lined up his putt and rolled it in for a bogey.

Richard pulled out an official PGA Tour ball marker that he placed in front of his ball. (C6.14) He then lifted, cleaned, and replaced his ball behind the marker saying, "My son bought me this when I took him to Firestone Country Club." He then stood over his line and stroked his ball for par.

Nicholas holed his putt in for bogey.

As Dick replaced his ball and picked up his marker, he drew a line with his finger on the green between his ball and the cup (C6.15), saying, "I just need to follow this path and I'm home." Addressing the ball, he stroked his putt for birdie. "And that's how you play under par," he said.

Chapter 6—Rules Explanations

C6.1—You are not allowed to change the characteristics of a club. That means you may not purposefully bend a club or attach anything to it. There's a two-stroke penalty for changing a club's characteristics or carrying an altered club. Using the club has its own penalty of disqualification. R#4-2b

C6.2—The ball must be teed inside the teeing area. The player can stand outside the area. If the ball is played outside the teeing area and the error is not corrected before playing from the next tee, the penalty is disqualification. R#11-4b

C6.3—When playing a provisional ball or another ball from the tee box, you should wait until everyone has hit their first ball before you play your second shot. There's no penalty for not following this rule as long as it's not done to give one of the players an advantage. R#10-3

C6.4—If a ball is visibly cut, cracked, or out of shape, it is unfit for play and can be replaced without penalty. R#5-3(1)

Remember, before lifting a ball, you must inform your competitor and mark it. Not informing your opponent or scorekeeper (marker) comes with a one-stroke penalty.

C6.5—If your ball had become unfit for play on the hole you are playing, you may substitute another ball, placing it on the spot where the original ball was. There is no penalty for replacing an unfit ball. R#5-3(2)

<u>C6.6</u>—Mud and scratches aren't enough to make a ball unfit. So picking up the ball, when not permitted, incurs a one stroke penalty. R#5-3(3)

<u>C6.7</u>—You are responsible for knowing the rules. That's the rule. R#6-1

<u>C6.8</u>—You are allowed to move loose impediments when not in a hazard. If your ball moves when you are moving impediments, there's a one-stroke penalty and you must replace your ball.

Loose impediments are natural objects, such as leaves, twigs, or bugs. They are not anything growing or fixed. R#23-1

<u>C6.9</u>—You are allowed, without penalty, to mark and lift your ball in order to identify it.

Replace it exactly where and how you found it. And remember to announce to your fellow competitor whenever you lift your ball when you're not on the putting green. Not doing so incurs a one stroke penalty. And you aren't allowed to clean it. R#12-2

<u>C6.10</u>—You are allowed to probe the water for your ball. If you accidentally move it, there's no penalty; just replace it. R#12-1c

<u>C6.11</u>—You are allowed to hit a ball that is moving in water without penalty. R#14-6

<u>C6.12</u>—You can drop your ball behind the water hazard, keeping the point where the ball entered the water in line with the hole. There's no limit to how far back you can go. Not dropping in the correct place will cost you a two-stroke penalty. R#26-1b

C6.13—You are allowed to lift your ball on the putting green without penalty after you mark it. Any marker can do as long as it doesn't interfere with other players. R#16-1b(1)

C6.14—You are allowed to mark your ball on any side of the ball as long as you replace your ball on the exact spot from where it was lifted. R#16-1b(2)

C6.15—The line for a putt may be pointed out, but in doing so, the green must not be touched. Touching the green anywhere incurs a two-stroke penalty. R#8-2b

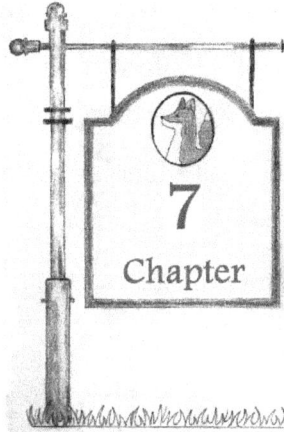

The seventh hole was a short island-style hole surrounded by water with a little piece of land as a bridge. The par-3 had a large, round green with a yard of deep rough surrounding it that would catch golf balls before they rolled off into the water.

"Watch this, girls," said Dick as he pulled his 8-iron from his bag and walked toward the tee box and dropped his ball on the ground. A smooth three-quarter swing sent his ball right at the flag. With a gentle thud, the sound every golfer loves to hear, his ball landed close to the hole.

"Nice shot," Richard said as he teed up for his shot. A full swing of his 9-iron landed him on the green too, ten feet from the hole.

Howard was next, landing his 9-iron just off the green in the rough.

"Where's Nicholas?" asked Howard, to which everyone started looking around. He was spotted two fairways over at a snack cart. They all watched him for several minutes until he arrived back, mouth full of chips (C7.1).

After some verbal abuse from the rest of the group for having to wait for him and for not bringing anything back to share, Nicholas teed off. His 8-iron landed short of the island, in the water.

"Serves you right," said Dick as Nicholas headed off.

Nicholas walked up to the drop zone, which was just to the left of the bridge to the green. Using his lob wedge from this short distance, he landed his replacement ball near the cup.

"Nice on," Richard said as he and the group walked the path to the green.

Howard stood for a long time looking at his ball as he didn't feel comfortable with lies like this.

Pulling out a pitching wedge, he finally swung as hard as he could. The long grass grabbed at his club, which slowed down the swing and opened the face. He made contact with the ball but not like he wanted. The ball went hard right and only a few yards but was now on the green.

Howard was still away, with a straight twenty-five-foot putt. Dick, in his usual helpful manner, stood just to the high side of Howard's line saying, "Run it just to my side," (C7.2) to which Howard stroked it on the line indicated into the cup. "Told you so," said Dick.

"Hey, Howard, which way do you think this will break (C7.3)?" asked Richard as he was squatting behind his ball and reviewing his putt.

"Looks like it's a half-hole to the right," replied Howard (C7.4).

Taking that line, Richard rolled his putt to an inch from the cup.

"Arm check," yelled Dick. "Did you forget to eat your cereal this morning?"

Not acknowledging the remark, Richard walked up to his ball and tapped in for par.

Nicholas walked up to his ball. He pulled out a handkerchief and wrapped it around his putter's grip (C7.5) in order to have a better grip because of his sweating hands. He made a nice stroke and sunk his putt to finish with a bogey.

Dick was only a foot away from the hole. He stood with the hole between him and his ball and dragged his putter toward the cup, pulling his ball into the hole (C7.6). "Damn, only a birdie. That should have been an ace," he said.

Chapter 7—Rules Explanations

C7.1—You should not be slow during play and between holes. This is called undue delay or slow play. You can be penalized two strokes for this behavior, but it's generally just considered poor etiquette. R#6-7

C7.2—You can't make a stroke with your partner or your caddie positioned on or close to an extension of the line of play. Add a two-stroke penalty to the player for doing so. This example is more of advice given (R#8-1), but you get the idea. R#14-2b

C7.3—You aren't allowed to ask for advice from anyone other than your partner, your caddie, or your partner's caddie. There's a two-stroke penalty for asking for help. R#8-1b

C7.4—You aren't allowed to *give* advice either. There's a two-stroke penalty for giving help. R#8-1a

C7.5—You must not use any artificial device or unusual equipment that might assist in gripping the club *except* gloves, powder, a towel, or a handkerchief. Using any unacceptable equipment in this manner results in a penalty of disqualification. R#14-3c(iii)

C7.6—You must fairly strike the ball with the head of the club, and the club must not be pushed, scraped, or spooned. A two-stroke penalty for doing so is imposed. R#14-1

8

Chapter

"I love this hole," Dick stated as he pulled his driver out of his golf bag and walked to the tee box of the dogleg par-5. "It's my favorite hole on the entire course. As a matter of fact, before you guys arrived this morning, I warmed up on this hole (C8.1). A buddy of mine works here and got me on the course before the facility opened."

Teeing his ball and making a solid swing, the ball flew down the fairway, landing in the center and rolling another forty yards. "You get a nice kick going down that hill if you place it right," Dick said with a grin as he picked up his tee.

Howard, Richard, and Nicholas then took their respective turns as they followed with their drives.

Richard's ball found the right side of the fairway in a hazard that was lightly covered with leaves.

Howard's shot landed on the right side of the fairway, shorter than Richard's, under a low hanging limb.

Nicholas's drive was straight down the middle. Happily, he picked up his tee and headed off toward his ball.

"I know it's here somewhere," Richard stated after reaching the hazard as he drug his wedge back and forth around the ground, searching for his ball under the leaves. Suddenly a click was heard as his club made contact with the ball still covered with leaves, moving it slightly (C8.2).

"Found it!" Richard said as he picked up the ball, glanced at it to verify his markings, replaced it on the ground, and covered it back up with leaves. Then, ever so gently, he picked a couple of leaves off the top so as to allow some of the white of his ball to be seen (C8.3). Addressing the ball, he took his swing and sent the ball back into the fairway at the beginning of the dogleg.

Howard walked back and forth under the tree several times, stopping periodically to try a different approach to clearly address his ball.

"I think I got it," Howard mumbled as he walked back to his bag, fished around his clubs, then pulled out a very old 3-iron. "This should do it," he said as he bent the hosel so the shaft could swing under the tree branch (C8.4).

Taking a long, slow backswing, he swung his club, and the head made clean contact, sending his ball near the end of the dogleg, leaving a nice approach to the green.

Nicholas's lie was good, sitting in the short grass. A smooth hybrid landed his ball near Richard's and Howard's.

Dick didn't have sight of the flagstick because of the dogleg, so he played a 7-iron to set himself up for a nice wedge to the green.

Everyone now had open shots to the secluded green on the right, guarded by trees to the back and the sides.

Dick hit a nice pitching wedge to put him on the green.

Howard too had a good lie but left himself twenty yards short of the green on a slightly uphill lie.

Nicholas had gone long and to the right, which put him on the side of the green, just on the fringe.

Richard played a nice 9-iron onto the green.

Standing over his ball, Howard took several perfect practice swings, but as he addressed the ball, he leaned back, obviously in an attempt to loft the ball, resulting in topping the ball, sending it only five yards forward.

Staring angrily at the spot where the ball was just lying, he pulled out another ball from his pocket and placed it exactly where his original ball had been.

"This is just practice (C8.5)," Howard said as he addressed the ball with proper positioning and, making solid contact, dropped the ball within four feet from the cup.

He then walked to his first ball and also chipped that close to the hole.

Nicholas, still off the green, chose to putt the ball and knocked it within a foot, which he then tapped in for par.

Richard two-putt for par, Howard made his putt for a nice up-and-down par, and Dick sank his putt for birdie.

"That's how you do it! This game is easy," Dick explained (<u>C8.6</u>).

Chapter 8—Rules Explanations

C8.1—You aren't allowed to practice or play on the same course before a competition in which you are competing. The penalty for breaking this rule is disqualification. R#7-1b

C8.2—In a bunker, you can, without penalty, move loose impediments in looking for your ball. If you move the ball, though, you incur a one-stroke penalty and must replace the ball and recreate the lie. R#12-1b(1)

C8.3—If you do move impediments to find your ball, you must replace the impediments - even if you have to cover your ball. You are allowed to leave a little of the ball showing, though. Failure to follow this rule results in a penalty of two strokes. R#12-1b(2)

C8.4—You cannot purposely change the characteristics of a club. By using an adjusted club, the penalty is disqualification. If the club is changed but not used then the penalty is two strokes for each hole the club is carried, with a maximum of four penalty strokes. R#4-2a

C8.5—You aren't allowed to practice during the play of a hole. You can practice chipping and putting on or near the green just played, the teeing ground of the next hole, or any practice area. Add a two-stroke penalty for breaking this rule. R#7-2

C8.6—The game of golf consists of playing a ball with a club from the teeing ground into the hole by a stroke, or successive strokes, in accordance with the rules. Sounds easy, huh? R#1-1

~ Richard E. Todd ~

9

Chapter

"Now this is my favorite hole," Richard said, looking at the par-3, 125-yard ninth hole. It played from an elevated tee box across a valley to a large green with sand to the left, a grass mound to the right, and trees behind.

Dick still had honors. He pulled out his pitching wedge, teed up a ball, waggled his club, and let it rip. The ball was on a perfect line for the hole. It landed three feet past the flag then started to roll back down the green toward the cup. The ball stopped on the edge of the cup, defying gravity, with part of the ball hanging into the air (C9.1). "Are you kidding me!" Dick yelled. "That's got to be an ace."

"We'll see if it drops in while the rest of us hit," Richard said as he took his turn, landing his shot on the right side of the green after a well-hit 9-iron.

Up next, Nicholas landed his tee shot on the front of the green.

"You're up, Howard," Richard said, then realized Howard wasn't near. Looking around, he noticed Howard was still on the last hole, practicing his chipping (C9.2).

"Hey, you're up," Dick yelled. "Get over here."(C9.3) To which Howard grabbed his golf bag and ran to the ninth tee box.

"Sorry," Howard said as he quickly teed up a ball and stroked it to the left side of the green.

As soon as everyone had teed off, Dick ran to the green and right up to the hole and yelled. "Drop, you stupid ball, drop," he said.

Dick yelled, jumped, and walked around the hole for a minute.

"Give it up. It's not going in," said Howard.

"Fine," grumbled Dick as he straddled his ball, as if he was playing croquet, and tapped it into the cup. (C9.4) "Birdie. That's how you do it."

Nicholas was next to putt out. He misjudged the slope of the green and left his putt five feet short.

Howard and Richard each took their respective turns, two-putting for par.

Nicholas lined up his par putt but left that short too. "Ugh," he said then tapped in for bogey.

Chapter 9—Rules Explanations

C9.1—If your ball hangs on the lip of the cup, you are allowed enough time to reach the hole without delay and an additional ten seconds. If the ball hasn't dropped in yet, it's considered "at rest." If it falls in after that time, it's as if it fell in with your last stroke, but also add a penalty of one stroke. R#16-2

C9.2—You are not allowed to practice during play of a hole. You can, between holes, practice putting or chipping on or near the putting green of the last hole played. Practicing when not allowed incurs a two-stroke penalty. R#7-2a

C9.3—You are allowed to practice chipping or putting on a hole you just finished as long as it does not delay play. R#7-2c

C9.4—You are not allowed to putt "astride" or with either foot touching the line of the putt. If you do putt like this example, add a penalty of two strokes. You can putt in this manner only if the purpose is to avoid standing on someone else's putting line. R#16-1e

10
Chapter

"Anyone need to grab something to eat at the clubhouse?" Richard asked although he knew, from golfing with these guys before, everyone liked to keep the momentum and pace of play going (C10.1).

At the tee box, Dick started his preshot routine and then let a nice drive fly down the left side of the fairway.

The par-4 tenth hole was 355 yards long, with trees to the left of the fairway, which opened at the end to reveal the protected green. The right side was fairly clear and open, with a few sparse trees to separate it from the fourteenth hole that was playing the opposite direction.

After a few practice swings, Howard addressed his tee shot and hit a major duck hook that went deep into the woods.

"Damn!" he yelled as he took his driver and smashed the tee box marker, cracking the club's face (C10.2).

"Way to hold your temper," Dick retorted.

Nicholas then took his turn. While taking a practice swing, his driver hit the ground, and the club head broke off, flying down the fairway. "Whoa!" he said.

"It's those hand-me-down clubs," stated Dick. "I told you last week you needed to upgrade."

"Can I borrow your driver?" Nicholas asked Richard (C10.3).

"Sure," replied Richard, who handed him the driver from his bag (C10.4).

"Thanks," said Nicholas as he promptly teed a ball and smashed his drive down the middle of the fairway. "Nice club," he said as he returned the driver to Richard.

Taking his stance, Richard also hit his drive down the middle although twenty yards farther. "Yup, nice club," he stated.

"I'll be right back," Howard grumbled as he began heading back toward the clubhouse, leaving his bag at the tee box.

"Yeah, me too," said Nicholas as he rushed off in the same direction.

"Okay," Richard and Dick responded as they started off toward their next shot.

Richard reached his ball first. He was 150 yards from the hole, with a clear path to the green. Taking a nice swing with his 8-iron, he landed on the front part of the green.

Dick played a smooth pitch from 135 yards and landed within ten feet of the cup.

"Incoming," yelled Howard, followed immediately by the sound of his driver making contact with his golf ball, then followed by the muffled thump as his shot landed in the fairway.

"Where did you go," asked Richard.

"Back to the clubhouse," Nicholas and Howard said in tandem.

"I went to get a new club," said Howard. (C10.5).

"Me too," Nicholas said.

Richard and Dick stood, shaking their heads, as they watched Nicholas and Howard heading down the fairway for their second shots.

Howard, hitting again, sent his ball on a low trajectory for the flagstick. It hit the fairway and rolled onto the putting green. "Not a pretty shot, but it got the job done," he said.

Promptly following Howard's shot was Nicholas, who just missed the green on the right side.

With everyone else on, Nicholas started to line up his chip shot, taking several pendulum-like practice swings, back and forth, back and forth. Finally addressing the ball, he took his shot. As the club made contact with the ball, there was an odd sound as the ball was sent up and softly landed near the cup.

With a puzzled look, Nicholas checked the ground where his ball had just been. He found a rock slightly protruding from the freshly made divot. It has been lying just beneath the grass.

"I hit a rock," he said.

"Any damage?" asked Richard as Nicholas examined his club.

"Yup, scratched the sole (<u>C10.6</u>)."

"I had that happen the day I purchased my irons," Richard said (<u>C10.7</u>). "It'll be fine."

With everyone on the green, each took their turns to putt out. Dick sank his putt for birdie. Nicholas one-putt and Richard two-putt, each for par, and Howard one-putt for bogey.

Chapter 10—Rules Explanations

C10.1—You must keep a good pace of play, even between holes. A penalty of two strokes can be assessed by the committee, but generally, this is more of an etiquette item. R#6-7, note 2

C10.2—If your club is damaged other than in normal use and it is now non-conforming or the playing characteristics have changed, it cannot be used nor can it be replaced. Doing either of these results in a penalty of disqualification. R#4-3b

C10.3—If your club is damaged in the normal course of play, you may repair or replace it. R#4-3a(iii)

C10.4—Partners may share clubs only if the combined total of clubs is not more than fourteen. Sharing clubs, if the total of both is more than fourteen clubs, incurs a two-stroke penalty for each hole that the rule was broken, with a maximum penalty of four strokes. R#4-4b

C10.5—You must not delay play when having a club repaired or replaced. The penalty for delaying play is disqualification. R#4-3a(ii)

C10.6—A club damaged during a round can still be used, but a scratched club isn't enough to deem it "damaged." R#4-3i

C10.7—You can use a club that was damaged before you started the round as long as the club still conforms to the rules. R#4-3c

~ Richard E. Todd ~

11

Chapter

"Looks like I'm up again," Dick said as he began heading to the tee box. "You gotta play this hole smart. That gully can add strokes quickly," he said, referring to the 425-yard par-4 eleventh hole that had a thirty-foot-wide ditch running across the fairway at 190 yards from the tee box and having a 225 carry.

Dick teed his ball, set himself, initiated a big turn, and made a monster swing, hitting the ball solid and sending it over the gully on a beautiful draw. "And that's how you do it," he said.

Knowing his drives aren't consistently that long, Richard played a 7-iron, landing in the middle of the fairway, fifteen yards short of the drop-off.

Nicholas also laid up, using his 5-iron to land his ball next to Richard.

"I'm going for it," Howard stated as he pulled out his driver and teed up his ball. Stepping up to the ball, Howard ripped it as hard as he could. The ball started for the left side of the fairway then ever so gently started sliding to the right toward the center of the fairway.

"I think it's going in," Dick said, as everyone watched the ball smash into the embankment just a few yards short of making it over the gully.

"Good luck getting out of there," Dick said as he started walking away.

Nicholas, still 250 yards from the hole, played his fairway hybrid. His shot was straight, and it landed in the fairway but well short of the green.

For his second shot, Richard took his 3-iron and placed his ball just short of the green.

Howard, assisted by Dick, trudged down the hill to look for Howard's ball.

"This might be it," Dick said as they both moved their heads close to the spot to examine a ball that was barely visible and embedded on the side of the gully.

"Yeah, it's mine, I see my mark," Howard stated. "But there's no way I can play the ball from this lie (C11.1), it's unplayable.

"Looks fine to me," Dick replied.

"Are you kidding? It's lodged in the dirt, totally buried," he said as he inched his fingers through the dirt around the ball to pull it out.

"There's no place around here to drop," Howard said (C11.2).

"Are you going back to the tee box?" asked Dick (C11.3).

Looking around, Howard said frustratingly, "I can't drop down here. I'm going back up to drop (C11.4)," to which he climbed back up and looked for a place to drop his ball.

This looks like a good spot, Howard thought, finding a grassy area to put his ball into play. *Let's just brush off this mud first* (C11.5)*, and get it to the green.* After a quick rub of the ball with his golf towel, Howard dropped the ball in a nice flat area. Taking out his rescue wood, he made his swing. After a solid swing and a lucky bounce, the ball rolled onto the green.

Dick, having cleared the gully on his drive, had 185 yards to the green. A smooth 6-iron put him solidly on.

Richard and Nicholas had short chips onto the green, which both dropped within five feet of the cup.

Once on the green, Howard was away. He took his time lining up his putt. While waiting, Dick walked around the green, repairing pitch marks from where balls had previously landed and left indentions on the grass (C11.6).

"Did you see my new divot repair tool?" Dick asked while not looking up but continuing to repair marks. "It's from St. Andrews, the birthplace of this ancient game."

"Excuse me! You moved my marker," yelled Richard.

"Sorry, just trying to repair the green," said Dick as he replaced Richard's marker (C11.7).

Howard finally putt, running a yard past the hole.

Dick lined up his putt and, with a smooth stroke, dropped it. "Birdie! And that's how you do it," he said.

Richard and Nicholas each made their putts for a nice up-and-down par while Howard tapped his ball back to the cup for bogey.

Chapter 11—Rules Explanations

C11.1—Only the player can decide if his ball is unplayable. Stating your ball is unplayable allows you to lift and either clean or substitute your ball and drop in an approved location for a one-stroke penalty. R#28

C11.2—One option is for you to drop within two club lengths of where the ball lay when it was determined to be unplayable. R#28c

C11.3—You can go back to where the ball was last played and hit again using the stroke and distance option for a one-stroke penalty. If using this option, count your first stroke, add a penalty stroke, and take your third shot. R#28a

C11.4—You can drop anywhere behind where your ball lay on a line to the flag. If using this option, you can lift, clean, and re-drop for a penalty of one stroke. Don't forget to count your first stroke too. R#28b

C11.5—You can clean your ball if calling for an unplayable lie. R#28

C11.6—You may repair old hole plugs and ball marks on the putting green even if your ball is not on the green. Don't repair any other damage to the green if the area to be fixed might assist you in playing the hole. R#16-1c(1)

<u>C11.7</u> —If you accidentally move a ball or ball marker in repairing the green, there is no penalty. Simply replace the marker in the original spot or as close as possible. R#16-1c(2)

12

Chapter

The twelfth hole was a 210-yard par-3 that had a straight fairway which sloped down to a large oval green surrounded by grassy bunkers on either side. The back edge rolled down to a pond that was filled with tall reeds.

Dick had honors and, making a gentle swing with his 6-iron, landed his tee shot ten yards from the hole.

"Nice shot, Dick," said Howard, "but how about you play from the white tees as we've been doing all day?" (C12.1)

Enjoying his birdie on the last hole, Dick wasn't paying attention and accidentally teed from the wrong set of tee boxes. Despite the extra ten yards, he executed a nice shot.

"Let's see if you can do that again from here," stated Howard, pointing to the white tee markers.

"You're just jealous," Dick retorted as he teed up another ball from the proper tee box and landed it even closer. "And that's how you do it," he said, walking off the tee-box.

Richard went next, playing a 5-iron just to the front of the green.

Nicholas played a 3-wood and rolled his shot onto the left side of the green.

Howard, with his fairway wood, landed on the right side of the green.

Richard then made a nice chip for his second shot, running his ball to within five feet of the hole.

With everyone on the green, Nicholas lined up his putt and stroked it.

Not paying attention, Howard also putt his ball at the same moment. Both balls were simultaneously racing to the hole from opposite sides of the green (C12.2).

Luckily, both balls stopped short of the hole.

"Sorry," said Howard as he walked up and tapped in his putt for par.

"It's okay," Nicholas replied as he too dropped his par putt.

Richard also rolled his putt in for par.

Dick holed his short putt for birdie. "Easy-peasy," he said as he picked up his ball out of the cup and headed to the next hole.

Chapter 12—Rules Explanations

<u>C12.1</u>—If you play from the wrong set of tees, you've effectively played from outside the teeing ground. If you don't correct your mistake before starting the next hole, you are disqualified. To correct your error, simply re-tee your ball in the proper teeing ground and play the hole. Any of the strokes made before the ball was properly put into play do not count, but a two-stroke penalty is added. R#11-5

<u>C12.2</u>—You are not allowed to make a stroke on the putting green while another ball is in motion. Doing so incurs a two-stroke penalty. There is no penalty if it was your turn to play and someone else hit. R#16-1f

~ Richard E. Todd ~

13

Chapter

"Okay, the thirteenth hole. Anyone feel lucky?" Dick said as he approached the tee box of the par-3. The hole played from an elevated tee box to a small green. The flagstick was in the front, and the green was surrounded by bunkers that were lower than the green itself, creating a high lip on the bunkers.

Playing 170 yards to the center, Dick pulled out his 6-iron, teed and played, and landed on the left side of the green.

"Not my best shot, but I'll take it," Dick said. "You're up, Howard."

Howard's drive ended on the backside of the green, in some deep rough on an uneven lie.

Richard's tee shot landed in the right side bunker.

Nicholas' first shot was short of the sand, still in the fairway, thirty yards from the green.

Once to his lie, Nicholas planned to fly his ball over the bunker to the narrow part of the green containing the hole—a high-risk shot.

"I need the ball to stop quick once it hits the green. That's going to require a lot of backspin. I think I'm gonna switch out my ball for one of those new high-spin models," Nicholas said to Richard (C13.1).

Nicholas reached down and picked up his ball and replaced the high-spin model for it (C13.2).

Opening up his stance for the shot, Nicholas took a big swing and slid his club into the ball, launching it high and landing it softly on the green. The ball hit the grass and immediately stopped just a foot from the hole.

"Yes!" he said as he pumped his fist in the air.

Howard found his ball in the rough. Taking his stance with his pitching wedge, he prepared to hit the ball out and onto the green. As he brought the club down on the ball, the grass greatly slowed the speed of his swing just as the club made contact with the ball. The club continued on its arc and made contact with the ball again, hitting it twice during his one stroke (C13.3). His shot did make it to the green but much shorter than desired, leaving a twenty-foot putt.

"That stunk," Howard said to himself as he walked out of the trap, rapping his club on his shoes to remove the sand.

Richard took his turn next. With an open stance and a smooth swing, he dropped his ball close to the hole.

"Nice out," Dick said as Richard walked to his ball.

Richard stood over his two-foot putt and rolled it toward the cup. The line looked good but lipped out, sending it a foot to the right.

"Oohhh," Howard said as Richard tapped in for bogey.

Howard then two-putt for bogey, Nicholas one-putt for par, and Dick one-putt for birdie.

Chapter 13—Rules Explanations

<u>C13.1</u>—You must hole out (that's the golf lingo for *finish*) with the ball played from the teeing ground. R#15-1

<u>C13.2</u>—You may substitute a ball only when a rule permits, such as for a lost or damaged ball. A two-stroke penalty is added for changing balls during play of a hole when not permitted. R#15-2

<u>C13.3</u>—If you hit the ball more than once during the same stroke, you don't have to count both contacts as strokes. Only count the first swing, then add a penalty of one stroke, for a total of two strokes. *This really does happen!* R#14-4

14
Chapter

"Well, this hole is trashed," Howard said as he looked out over the par-4 fourteenth hole.

"It's a work in progress," stated Dick. "They're widening the fairway . . ."

"Right, I can see the tree stumps running the length of the left side of the fairway," replied Howard.

"Increasing the drainage . . ."

"Oh, that's not a creek running across the middle of the fairway?"

"Building a bunker to the right . . ."

"That's what the pile of sand is for?"

"And enhancing the putting area."

"I wondered why there was a bulldozer near the green."

"Whatever," said Dick, as he turned toward his bag, fished out a tee, and headed toward the tee box. "I have honors again."

A quick setup, a waggle, and a swing put his drive down the middle of the fairway, coming to rest with a splash in the standing water around the plugged drain.

"Right, nice conditions," Howard said as he teed up his ball and promptly pulled his drive. His ball was heading toward the left side of the fairway. It directly hit one of the stumps then ricocheted around the others like a pinball. "Real nice hole," he said again as he picked up his tee and trudged off the tee box.

Next up was Richard, who faded his drive. It landed near the end of the fairway then rolled into the in-progress bunker on the right.

"I'm starting to agree with you, Howard," Richard said.

Nicholas's drive was straight and stopped in the center of the fairway, short of the water.

Richard came upon the bunker but couldn't find his ball through the bags of sand. "It's got to be here," he said and began to move the sandbags and feel around them.

"There you are," said Richard as his finger brushed the ball, causing it to roll out from under the stacks (C14.1).

"Looks like the groundskeeper stopped early," Richard said as he picked up his ball and dropped it in a completed section of the bunker (C14.2). Grabbing a wedge, he hit the ball out, landing it at the fifty-yard marker.

Nicholas found his ball in a good lie. Taking his fairway wood, he hit it onto the green, but it was moving too fast and rolled off the back.

"Good thing I'm wearing my new super water-resistant Feet-Glad golf shoes, otherwise my toes would be soaked. I just picked these up at the Grandé Golf store," Dick said as he gingerly stepped through the puddles to reach his ball. Carefully he picked up the submerged ball, flicked his hand to remove some mud and excess water from it, walked back out of the water, and dropped the ball into play in the nearest dry spot (C14.3). Playing his 7-iron, he landed his shot on the green.

Howard reached the stump area. From the tee-box he could not see that the area was encircled by a white line, painted on the ground, to mark the area as ground under repair. After sufficient time looking, he was unable to find his ball amid the pieces of bark, holes, and remains of once-tall pines.

"Remind me to thank the greenskeeper for his work on this hole," stated Howard as he rummaged in his golf bag for a replacement ball (C14.4). Taking a step to the side of the stumps, he dropped a replacement ball and began to play through, landing his ball short of the green.

Continuing on, Howard found that his second shot had landed in a mushy area short of the green and embedded in its own pitch mark.

Once to his lie, still grumbling, Howard took his wedge and scooped the ball out of the divot. He grabbed the ball and dropped it just behind the divot (C14.5). Trying to keep his feet clean, he took a one-legged stance and pitched his ball onto the green. Adding further insult, he splattered mud on his pant legs with his swing.

Richard, while chuckling at the sight, also pitched onto the green.

Nicholas, being just off the collar, putt with his 7-iron to knock it close to the hole. He then walked onto the green to meet the others.

In a never-ending streak of bad luck, Howard found his ball in an area, a foot wide and running the full length of the putting green, that had no grass, just dirt. Apparently, this was an area yet to be sodded.

"Are you kidding me?" Howard yelled upon sight of his lie as he looked at everyone.

"This is becoming a habit for you," Dick stated as Howard, once again, picked up his ball and placed it at the nearest piece of actual sod (C14.6).

Being away, Howard putted but came up short. He gave a small grunt of exasperation as he marked his ball and waited for his turn to putt out.

Richard and Nicholas, with simple and short putts, sank their balls for par while Dick continued with his birdie streak.

"And that's the way you do it," Dick stated.

With a scowl, Howard placed his ball by his marker and holed out for a bogey.

"I think your bad luck is growing," Richard said as he motioned to the sky, pointing at the several very dark clouds rolling in.

Chapter 14—Rules Explanations

C14.1—In searching for your ball within an obstruction or abnormal ground condition, if you accidentally move it, there is no penalty. Furthermore, you are entitled to relief or you can replace the ball and play it as it lies. R#12-1d

C14.2—You are allowed relief from abnormal conditions, but if the ball is in a hazard then you must drop the ball in the hazard. R#25-1b(ii)(a)

C14.3—In an abnormal ground condition, you may lift and drop the ball without penalty within one club length of relief and not closer to the hole. R#25-1b(i)

C14.4—If you are certain your ball is in an abnormal ground condition but can't find it, relief can be obtained. Drop where the ball last crossed the outermost limits of the abnormal condition without penalty. R#25-1c(i)

C14.5—A ball in its own pitch mark in any closely mown area can be lifted, cleaned, and dropped without penalty. It must be dropped as near as possible to the spot it was embedded, but not nearer the hole. R#25-2

C14.6—In abnormal ground conditions on the putting green, you may lift and replace your ball without penalty at the nearest point of relief. R#25-1b(iii)

~ Richard E. Todd ~

15
Chapter

The fifteenth hole was a narrow but straight par-4 lined with trees and playing to an elevated green. Dick played his 3-wood to lessen the chance of an out-of-bounds drive. A smooth swing and solid contact placed his opening shot in the middle of the fairway, just 130 yards from the green.

"Nice shot," Richard said as he teed up and swung his 3-iron, landing twenty yards past Dick's ball.

"Back atcha," Dick replied.

Nicholas wasn't about to play it safe and pulled out the driver. A technically beautiful swing landed his drive just in the fairway, right and twenty yards short of Dick's.

Howard, feeling the need for some comeback action, pulled out the big stick also. A little too much draw on his drive landed his ball in the right rough under some low-hanging branches.

"Where's the hole? I can see the green but not the flagstick," Nicholas said, standing behind his ball, preparing for his second shot.

Dick walked behind Nicholas, placed his arm over Nicholas' shoulder, and pointed to the flag (C15.1). After holding the pose quietly for ten seconds, he withdrew his hand and headed toward his ball.

Using his 5-iron, Nicholas put the ball on the green.

Dick played next. He took his stance, ground his club right behind the ball, and ever so lightly, accidentally made contact with the ball, moving it a hair forward.

Damn, Dick thought. *That's a penalty stroke. I'll have to remember to tell Richard about that* (C15.2). Setting aside that event and being the optimal distance from the hole, he took his swing and landed his 9-iron shot on the green.

Howard, walking down the cart path, found his ball firmly at the base of a tree, lying between some exposed roots.

"Not again," Howard yelled as he threw his hands up in the air. "It's going to take me a couple strokes to get out of this lie. I'm taking a free drop."

"No, you don't get a free drop. You need to play it or take a penalty stroke and drop," Richard stated.

"I think you're wrong," Howard said coolly.

"I'm pretty sure I'm right," Richard replied. "Why don't you play two balls until we can clarify it at the clubhouse? (C15.3) Play your first ball as it lies, and a second the way you think the rule is defined with a free drop."

"That's too much work," Howard said. "I'll just play this terrible lie. But I'm getting a different club," he said as he walked back to his golf bag and fished out a beat-up old wedge. "If I gotta play this lie, and possibly break a club, I'm gonna use trusty Rosie here, my old wedge," he said as he lifted the club.

"I think you should call it Rusty Rosie. Is that club legal?" Richard asked. "It looks pretty mangled." (C15.4)

"Yeah, it's fine," Howard muttered as he raised the wedge and brought it down on the ball, managing to propel it out, and onto the fairway.

"You better get your game in order," Dick said over some distant thunder. "Those shots are gonna bring a bad-luck storm."

Howard, still being his turn and taking the same club, pitched his ball onto the green then gave Dick a little smirk.

Last to shoot for the green was Richard. A nice 9-iron put him on with everyone else.

On the green, Howard lined up his twenty-foot putt and stroked it into the cup for par.

"Some of his luck is returning, but the sky is still looking dark," Dick said.

Richard was up next but left his putt short.

"Maybe the bad luck is moving to you," Dick said to Richard.

Richard then tapped in his putt for par.

Nicholas lined up his putt, but Dick's ball was directly in his path.

"Will you mark your ball?" Nicholas said to Dick.

"No way. Putt around me. It's not like you're going to make it anyhow," Dick said. (C15.5)

"Fine," Nicholas said as he lined up his putt and hit it on a path just outside Dick's ball. As expected, it stopped just to the side of the cup.

"Told ya," Dick said as he putted his ball in the hole for another birdie.

Nicholas walked over and tapped in his putt for par.

"Anyone else feel rain?" Richard asked as the wind picked up.

Chapter 15—Rules Explanations

C15.1—You may have the line of play indicated to you before your stroke. You may not have someone positioned so they are showing you the line while making a stroke. You may also not place an item on the course to show you the line. If you break the rule the penalty is two strokes. R#8-2a

C15.2—If you incur a penalty stroke, you are to inform your fellow competitor or marker as soon as practicable. R#9-3

C15.3—When in doubt as to the rule, you are allowed to play two balls: play one the way the ball lies, and play the other the way you think the rules allow you to. Before you play either ball, though, you must state to your competitors which shot is your preferred ball for your score. Once you can confirm the proper rule for that situation, you then take the score for the appropriate ball played. R#3-3a

C15.4—Any club that conformed when purchased is considered to be conforming as long as the wear is through normal use and not purposefully altered. R#4-1b

C15.5—If you refuse to follow a rule that affects the rights of a fellow-competitor then you are disqualified. R#3-4

.

~ Richard E. Todd ~

The par-5 sixteenth hole is normally a beautiful sight. It has a wide fairway with one huge oak tree right in the middle. Pine trees line the left side of the fairway and a wildflower-filled hillside is to the right. The fairway narrows after the oak as it takes a gentle bend to the right, reaching a large green surrounded by grass mounds and sand. But the clouds partially blocked the sun and turned everything a shade of gray.

"Just a few holes left, boys. We better get on our horses before we need boats. I'm up first again," Dick said as he hurried to plant a tee. He hit a solid drive, but the wind picked up and pushed the ball to the left side of the fairway. "That wind is really blowing," he said.

Richard quickly teed up his shot and landed it down the right side of the fairway.

Howard followed suit and landed his drive near Richard's.

Nicholas teed his ball and, after a quick waggle, started his backswing. Just as his club made contact with the ball, sending it down the center of the fairway, the air was electrified as a loud boom of thunder was heard.

"Whoa! Take cover!" yelled Howard as he ran toward a nearby shelter.

"Relax," Dick said, "that thunder was a long way off, and I didn't see any lightning. Let's press on." (C16.1)

With a brisk pace, each person played their second shots, moving the balls closer to the green. Richard and Howard were near the left side of the fairway while Nicholas and Dick were sitting in the middle of the fairway near the one-hundred-yard marker.

All the while, the air began to build with electricity.

Howard was away and standing over his ball just as the sky lit up.

"That's it! I'm not gonna get fried," he said (C16.2) as he grabbed his ball and golf bag and ran toward the shelter (C16.3).

Nicholas followed Howard, leaving his ball on the course (C16.4).

Richard grabbed the tee from behind his ear and stuck it in the ground as he picked up his ball, stuffed it in his pocket, and also ran off toward the shelter.

Dick calmly pulled out a PGA-branded raincoat from his golf bag and put it on. He then grabbed a nearby stick and forced it into the ground next to his ball, picked his ball up, and headed in the same direction.

Everyone reached the shelter just as the rain came pouring down.

***

They stood under the shelter, elbow to elbow as if in an elevator, pushing toward the center to avoid the rain that was blowing in.

"Why don't they have sides on these things?" Nicholas asked.

"To give us more dry space," replied Dick sarcastically.

"Anyone have a deck of cards?" asked Nicholas, to which there was no reply.

Everyone just continued to look at the rain coming down.

For some time, the only sounds were the drops of rain hitting the roof, an occasional distant clap of thunder, and the shuffling of feet.

"So a priest, a rabbi, and a lawyer are out golfing," interrupted Dick.

"Give me a break," said Howard.

"It's been a while since we heard thunder. Let's give it another five minutes and see if it stops raining," Richard said.

"I'm about ready to just continue playing. If you want to just sit here, I'll play ahead," Dick said. (C16.5)

"Hold on, I think it's letting up. Give it another couple minutes," Richard said.

Several more minutes passed as the rain slowed to just a few occasional drops.

"Good enough for me. Let's finish this up," said Dick as he took the first steps from under the shelter toward where his ball had been, the rest of the group following.

Dick reached the area he had been only to find several other branches blown down by the wind and rain in the general area he had placed his stick but found none sticking up.

"I know I left a stick here, so I'm not taking a penalty," Dick said. He moved several of the branches and looked at the ground for a clear area, then placed a new ball on the ground. (C16.6) Taking a nice swing with his wedge, his ball settled toward the back of the green.

Richard, unable to find his tee, placed a new ball in the area he felt he had been. (C16.7) Then, taking his 9-iron, he stroked his ball, settling a few yards off the left side of the green.

Howard walked to the area he had been before picking up his ball. Standing in one place, he spun around as he wore a confused look. Unsure where his ball had been, he placed another ball using his best guess of location then played a 9-iron onto the green.

Nicholas's ball was right where he left it. He marked it, picked it up, cleaned it on his pant leg, and put it back (C16.8). A swoosh of his 8-iron and his ball was on the green with the others.

At his ball, Richard easily chipped on the green, yet leaving himself a fifteen-foot putt.

The greens were now wet and slow, causing putts to not roll as well as they had. No birdies were to be had as everyone two-putt. Richard finished with a bogey, and the rest of the group made par.

Chapter 16—Rules Explanations

C16.1—You must not discontinue play unless there's a good reason or the committee or golf course tells you to stop playing. Bad weather is not considered a good reason to stop play. Stopping without approval is grounds for disqualification. R#6-8a(iv)

C16.2—You are allowed to stop playing if you believe there is danger from lightning. R#6-8a(ii)

C16.3—You must mark your ball before lifting it. If you lift without marking, then add a one-stroke penalty. R#6-8c(1)

C16.4—You are not required to lift your ball when discontinuing play. You can leave it on the course. R#6-8c(2)

C16.5—You must remain with your group throughout the round. Leaving your group will disqualify you. R#6-3b

C16.6—If your ball or ball marker is moved, you must estimate where the ball was and place it on that spot without a penalty. R#6-8d(iii, note)

C16.7—If your ball or ball-marker is moved (including by wind or water) while play is discontinued, a ball or ball-marker must be placed on the original spot. R#(6-8d(iii))

C16.8—After play is resumed, if you didn't mark and lift your ball prior, you may do so now since you were allowed to do so originally. R#6-8d(ii)

~ Richard E. Todd ~

17

Chapter

A unique hole, the seventeenth was a 333-yard par-4 that started from a heavily wooded and narrow tee box that slowly opened to a large area, then played up a 120-yard hill to a round green surrounded by closely growing maple trees.

Dick teed first, followed by Howard, Richard, and then Nicholas. Each successfully played easy swings off the tee and through the narrow opening into the fairway, glad that their shots stayed out of the woods.

"Everyone looks good," Richard said as they headed down the fairway for their second shots.

As they came to the clearing, they saw cleanup work being performed near the edge of the tree line where Nicholas's ball rested. As they approached the ball, a branch was thrown from one of the mowers, hitting Nicholas's ball and moving it a couple yards. (C17.1)

"Glad I wasn't closer, I better play this quick," Nicholas said as he ran to his ball, picked it up, moved the stick, placed the ball back on the spot it had been before it was moved, and proceeded to hit it toward the green. His shot was online but landed short and came to rest on the steep hill, twenty yards from the green.

Howard was next to hit, and the group congregated around his ball.

As Howard was lining up his shot, Richard's golf bag tipped over, clubs spilling out and hitting Howard's ball. (C17.2)

"Dude, what gives?" Howard said.

"Sorry, my bad," Richard apologized as he picked up his clubs while Howard placed the ball back to its original location then pitched it nicely onto the green.

"Nice one," Richard said.

"Thanks," Howard replied.

Richard had an open shot to the green and started pulling out an 8-iron.

"Why don't you drop your bag on his ball?" Dick said to Howard loud enough for all to hear.

Richard gave Dick a sideways look then pitched his ball toward the green.

"Looks short," Dick said as everyone watched the ball heading up the hill, landing on the hillside and producing two balls bouncing up. (C17.3)

"You don't see that every day. I think you hit Nicholas's ball," Dick said as he walked up to his ball, took an easy swing, and landed his shot on the green.

Moving up the hill, Richard reached his lie first. The grass was longer but manageable.

"Hey, Howard, can you lift the flag up? I can't see it from this angle," Richard said. Howard responded by walking over to the hole, pulling out the flagstick from the cup, and lifting it into the air. (C17.4)

"Okay, got it. You can put it back in," Richard said then took his pitching wedge and dropped the ball on the green.

Nicholas, finding his ball, stated his intention to move it two yards to the left, to the general area it was before Richard's ball moved it. (C17.5) Holding his arm out, he dropped his ball. Playing his lob wedge, he smoothly landed the ball on the green.

"You're away," Richard said to Nicholas.

"I think you're farther out," Nicholas replied.

"We'll see," responded Richard as he started measuring the distance from his ball to the hole, slowly putting one foot in front of the other, heel to toe, as he counted out loud. "Twenty-two for me," he said as he started pacing from the cup to Nicholas's ball.

"Twenty, oops, sorry," Richard said as his toe bumped Nicholas's ball and sent it rolling. (C17.6)

"I'll just go," Nicholas said in disgust as he darted a step, grabbed his ball, and placed it where it had been before it was moved.

Nicholas then stroked the ball within a foot of the cup. He then addressed and tapped in his ball.

Richard two-putt, tying with Nicholas for bogey, while Dick and Howard two-putt for par to finish the hole.

Chapter 17—Rules Explanations

C17.1—You are allowed to replace your ball at the original spot without penalty, since it was at rest and moved by an *outside agency*. (That's golf lingo again. An outside agency is any agency other than your fellow-competitors, or your fellow-competitor's caddies, any ball played by your fellow-competitor at the hole being played, or any equipment of your fellow-competitors. It also includes an observer, a marker, or a referee, and a forecaddie. It does not include wind nor water.) R#18-1

C17.2—If a competitor or his equipment moves your ball and you know the exact location, just replace the ball. There is no penalty. If the location isn't exactly known then drop the ball. R#18-4

C17.3—If your ball is at rest and moved by another ball, just replace your ball at the original spot it was before it was moved. There is no penalty for replacing it. R#18-5

C17.4—You can have someone hold the flagstick up in the air to indicate the location of the hole. It can even be held up while a stroke is being made. R#17-1

C17.5—If the spot your ball was at can't be specifically determined, simply drop as near as possible to the general location. R#20-3c

C17.6—If a ball or ball marker is moved while measuring, just replace the ball. There is no penalty. R#18-6

~ Richard E. Todd ~

18

Chapter

"Last hole, gents. Honors for me one last time," Dick said as he teed a ball and prepared for his drive.

The eighteenth hole was beautifully designed—a 550-yard par-5, starting as an open and flat fairway lined with trees. Eventually, the fairway went down a steep hill, across a small creek, and finished as a gradual uphill fairway to a large green with trees on both sides. Behind the green, you could see the clubhouse veranda perched high on the continuing uphill path. The patio was filled with golfers looking down at the fairway and green and anyone playing the final hole. There was no doubt why this was the course's signature hole.

Dick's drive came to rest just on the right edge of the fairway near the trees.

Richard's final drive landed in the middle of the fairway, just short of the hill.

Nicholas's drive came to rest near Richard's ball, and Howard's hooked toward the left side of the fairway.

Richard and Nicholas reached their drives first.

"Trying to show me up?" Richard said to Nicholas, pointing at the ground to show the two balls just inches from each other. "You're the back one."

"I can't hit my ball without hitting yours too. Would you mark it?" Nicholas said to Richard.

"Sure. Okay if I just go first? I've got enough space that I won't hit your ball," Richard asked. (C18.1)

"Have at it," replied Nicholas.

Richard, playing his much loved 5-iron, took a steep swing and knocked his ball across the creek without disturbing Nicholas's lie, leaving it 150 yards from the green.

"Nice," Nicholas said as he grabbed his 3-wood and sent his ball over the water too, landing on the right side of the fairway.

"Back at ya," Richard said.

From across the fairway, Dick yelled, "Nicholas, come over here and hold this branch out of the way while I knock this baby up close to the green" (C18.2)

Nicholas ran across the fairway and held back some branches from brushing against Dick while he hit a great 3-wood, landing fifty yards short of the green.

Howard found his ball just off the fairway and resting on the cart path. He picked up his ball, inspected it to assure it was his and was playable. Finding his normal three-dot pattern and the ball still in good condition, he dropped it just to the right of the road on the fairway. (C18.3)Pulling out his 3-wood, he stroked it down the fairway. As he watched the flight of his shot heading over the water, he saw two kids in a golf cart speeding across multiple fairways. A feeling in his gut foretold the future as he watched his ball land in front of the cart and, without noticing, the kids ran over his ball, causing it to be thrown twenty yards into the deeper rough. (C18.4)

"Thanks a lot!" Howard yelled at the youths as he started down the hill.

Howard finally came to his ball. Still 130 yards out, he took his 8-iron and landed the ball on the green.

Richard, Nicholas, and Dick all took their turns and pitched their balls on the green as well.

Nicholas was away and first up to putt. He addressed his ball and rolled it toward the hole, but it ran five feet past.

"Yikes," Dick said as he crouched down and marked his ball. "The greens have gotten fast," he said as he pulled a tube of lip balm from his pocket and applied some to his ball. "This helps slow down the roll," he said to puzzled looks from the rest of the group (C18.5). He then took his stance and stroked his ball firmly into the cup. "And that's how you do it. Birdie, to finish the round for me."

Howard and Richard each two-putt to finish with pars.

Nicholas knocked his ball back to the hole to complete the round with a par also.

"Hurry up and total the scores. I want to see how bad I beat you girls," Dick said as he put away his putter and started to head back to the clubhouse. "Oh, by the way, I had a penalty stroke back on the fifteenth I forgot to tell you about. (C18.6) So add one more to my score for that hole. I'm sure I still beat everyone."

"We'll see," Richard said as he stuffed his putter in his golf bag and started adding the scores and marking down totals as he followed the group.

Chapter 18—Rules Explanations

C18.1—If your ball lies in the path of another player's path of play and you are asked to move your ball, you must. You may play first instead of moving your ball; it's your choice. But you can't lift your ball if another ball is moving and may hit it. Lifting while another ball is in motion is a two-stroke penalty. R#22-2

C18.2—You are not allowed to make a stroke while someone is providing physical help or protection from the elements. There is a two-stroke penalty for doing so. R#14-2a

C18.3—You are allowed relief from an immovable obstruction, such as a cart path, as long as the ball does not lie in a water or lateral hazard. Without penalty, you must drop the ball within one club length of the nearest point of relief (that's golf lingo for *clear area*) but not closer to the hole. R#24-2a

C18.4—If your ball, while moving, is accidentally deflected or stopped by an outside agency, there is no penalty and the ball must be played as it lies. This is what is called a rub of the green, which means "luck" (bad or good). R#19-1

C18.5—You must not apply any foreign material to your ball. Doing so results in disqualification. R#5-2

C18.6—After finishing the round, the player should check his scores with the marker and settle any doubtful points before it is signed by himself and the marker and turned in to the Committee. Penalty for not doing this is disqualification. R#6-6b

~ Richard E. Todd ~

19
Chapter

"Get a look at her," Dick said, nodding his head toward the waitress at the other end of the patio. "That's over-the-top apparel," he said, remarking at the PGA brand polo she wore, draped by a USGA sweater, further accented by her pink Dockers and a pair of Sperrys. "Hey, honey. Can we get some service over here?"

"So how bad did I beat you?" Dick asked, looking over at Richard, who had his head bent over the scorecard, still adding and marking totals.

"Just about done," Richard replied.

"Hey, guys, I'm Christine. Have a good round?" the waitress asked.

"What do you think? Look at these mopes I had to golf with," replied Dick. "I'll take a tall draft."

"And for the rest of you?" asked Christine.

"Arnold Palmer for me," Nicholas said.

"Me too," Richard said as he continued to scribble.

"Draft here," Howard said.

"Be right back," Christine said as she turned and headed inside.

"I love this," Howard said, holding his arms up to reference the beautifully manicured surroundings. "The fresh air, a good walk, and finishing it up with a cold drink."

"Wow, did you see that?" said Nicholas, pointing back to the eighteenth green. "That guy just chipped it in from the one-hundred-yard marker."

From the clubhouse, you could see several fairways coming in and heading out.

"Okay, I have your answer," Richard said. (C19.1) "It was a real close game. In regular strokes, I had a 74, Howard had 74, and Nicholas had 74."

"I know I beat that," Dick said.

"Right," Richard replied. "In regular strokes, you had a 57."

"YES!" Dick yelled. "I told you I would win."

"Hold on," Richard said. "Let's factor in a few penalty strokes."

"Penalty strokes," Dick shouted. "What do you mean? Did I have any? Oh, that one back on 15?"

"That and a few others I've been tracking," Richard replied.

"Howard had 24 penalty strokes and two disqualification penalties, I had 10 penalty strokes, Nicholas had 8 penalty strokes—"

"Whoa, you guys need to learn the rules," Dick blurted out.

"And you had 32 penalty strokes, Dick," Richard said. "Oh, and you had five disqualification penalties. That nets you with a score of 89 and disqualified. Howard netted out at 100—"

"Isn't that a new low for you?" Dick asked.

"I had 84, and Nicholas had the low score of 82," Richard stated.

"YES!" yelled Nicholas as he jumped up and strutted around the table.

"Sit down, kid," Dick said. "It's only a game."

"Congrats, Nicholas," Richard said. "Good round."

"So who wants to play next week?" Dick asked. "Maybe a skins match?"

Chapter 19—Rules Explanations

<u>C19.1</u>—You may not make any changes to your scores after the card is turned in to the committee. R#6-6c

You probably aren't playing in a sanctioned tournament, rather just enjoying some golf with friends. But these are the rules of golf and are important to understand. Knowing them can make the game less frustrating and more equitable between all players, regardless of skill level.

You must follow the rules, that's the rule.

~ Richard E. Todd ~

The Golf Rules

Are you interested in learning more about the rules of golf, other playing formats, golf etiquette, or just want to enjoy another round with this group? Watch for future releases in the *The Golf Rules* book series.

Read *The Rules of Golf* and *Decisions on the Rules of Golf* by the USGA for even more in-depth information on golf rules.

This publication is not approved, sponsored, or endorsed by The United States Golf Association, and the USGA does not warrant the accuracy of the author's interpretations.

www.TheGolfRules.com

Rules reviewed by Bryan D. Lewis, USGA Committee Member/Rules Official
Author photo by Hannah E Todd, Instagram @HannahsMyName
Chapter artwork by Amber Christy
Cover photo by Michal Bednarek,

~ Richard E. Todd ~

Other titles from The Golf Rules…

The Golf Rules

Learn the rules of golf by watching others break them,

a humorous story focusing on stroke play format.

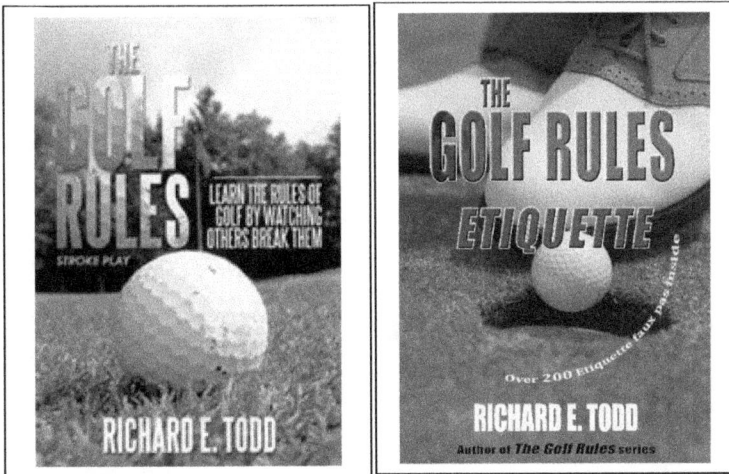

The Golf Rules-Etiquette

Enhance your golf etiquette by watching others' mistakes,

follow a municipal golfer on a country club course.

~ Richard E. Todd ~

Other titles available…

Short Stories from the Long Links

A collection of golf related tales.

Volume & 2

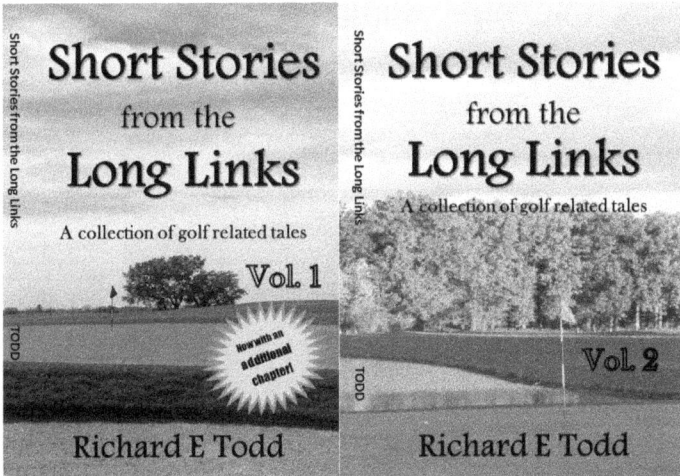

~ Richard E. Todd ~

Other titles available…

Design Your Own Golf Course Sketchpad

Design the perfect course with just the stroke of a pencil.

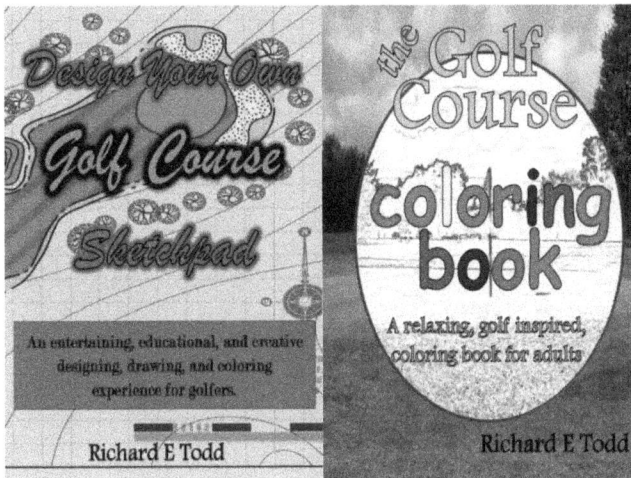

A Golf Course Coloring Book

A golf inspired, adult coloring book.

DEDICATION

To every golfer,
regardless of handicap, age, or frequency of play;
who, when not playing the game, enjoys watching it, talking about it,
dreaming about it, or reading related stories.

For more golf-related books and stories, links to follow me on
Facebook, Twitter, WordPress, and YouTube, and to learn more
about the author and upcoming and past events, visit
www.TheGolfRules.com.

I'd love your feedback! Please post a <u>review</u> on Amazon.

Follow on
Facebook, Twitter, WordPress, YouTube,
and on our website.

www.**AuthorRichardETodd**.com

www.**TheGolfRules**.com

I'd love your feedback! Please post a <u>review</u> on Amazon.

Follow on
Facebook, Twitter, WordPress, YouTube,
and on our website.

www.**AuthorRichardETodd**.com

www.**TheGolfRules**.com